Patterns on Purpose

By Allison Eley

Thank You, my King, for the wonders You've made—
for cycles and contrast in sunlight and shade,
for spirals in shells and the stars' steady spin,
for patterns that shout of Your truth deep within.

A heart on each
page is placed in view
among the patterns made for you—
in fingerprints and starry skies,
in buzzing bees and dragonflies.
The Creator formed both big and small
with wisdom woven through it all.
So search each page—look all around—
His love is everywhere
to be found!

ELEY
PUBLISHING
AVA, MISSOURI

"For by Him all things were
created, in heaven and on
earth, visible and invisible … all
things were created through
Him and for Him."

Colossians 1:16

For all of my
grandbabies—treasures so dear—
made by the Creator who holds you so near.
He fashioned the stars and framed the seas
and patterned the petals and sculpted the trees.
From snowflakes and seasons to songs that birds sing,
there's purpose and beauty in each little thing.
So marvel, my loves, at the world all around—
in rhythm and shape, His wonders are found.
They're really not random.
They're carefully planned.
Just like you—formed by His hand.
With all my love,
Mimi

"And God said,
'Let there be lights in the expanse
of the heavens to separate the day from
the night. And let them be for signs and
for seasons, and for days and years.'"
Genesis 1:14

(signs and seasons, days and years
to know His appointed times)

"He made the moon
to mark the seasons;
the sun knows its time
for setting."

Psalm 104:19

MOON PHASES

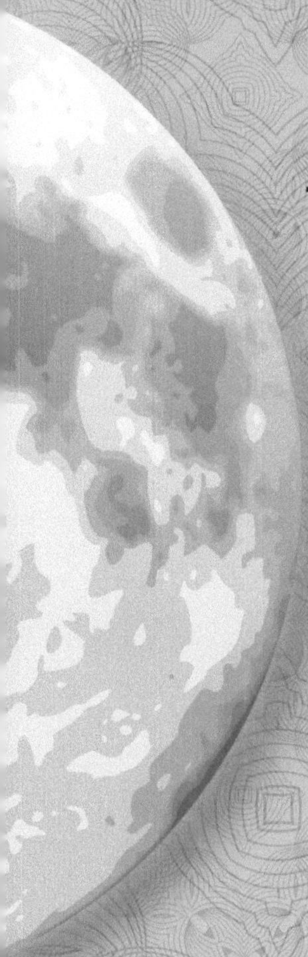

The moon keeps time up in the skies—
a calendar before our eyes!
With every phase, both dark and light,
it marks the season, day, and night.

Each cycle tells a tale so wise,
of order written in the skies!

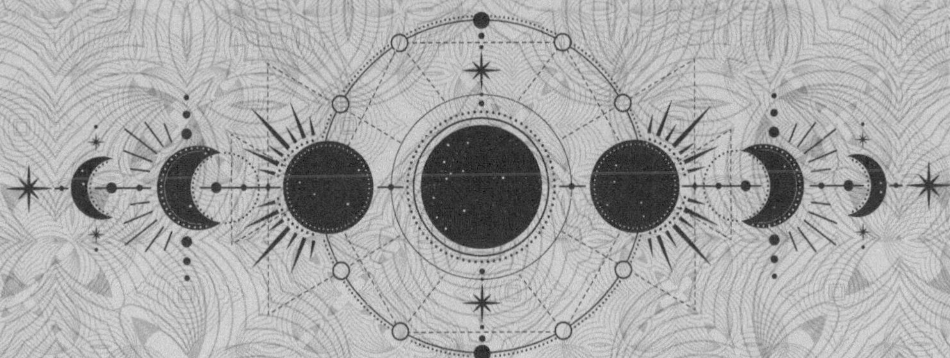

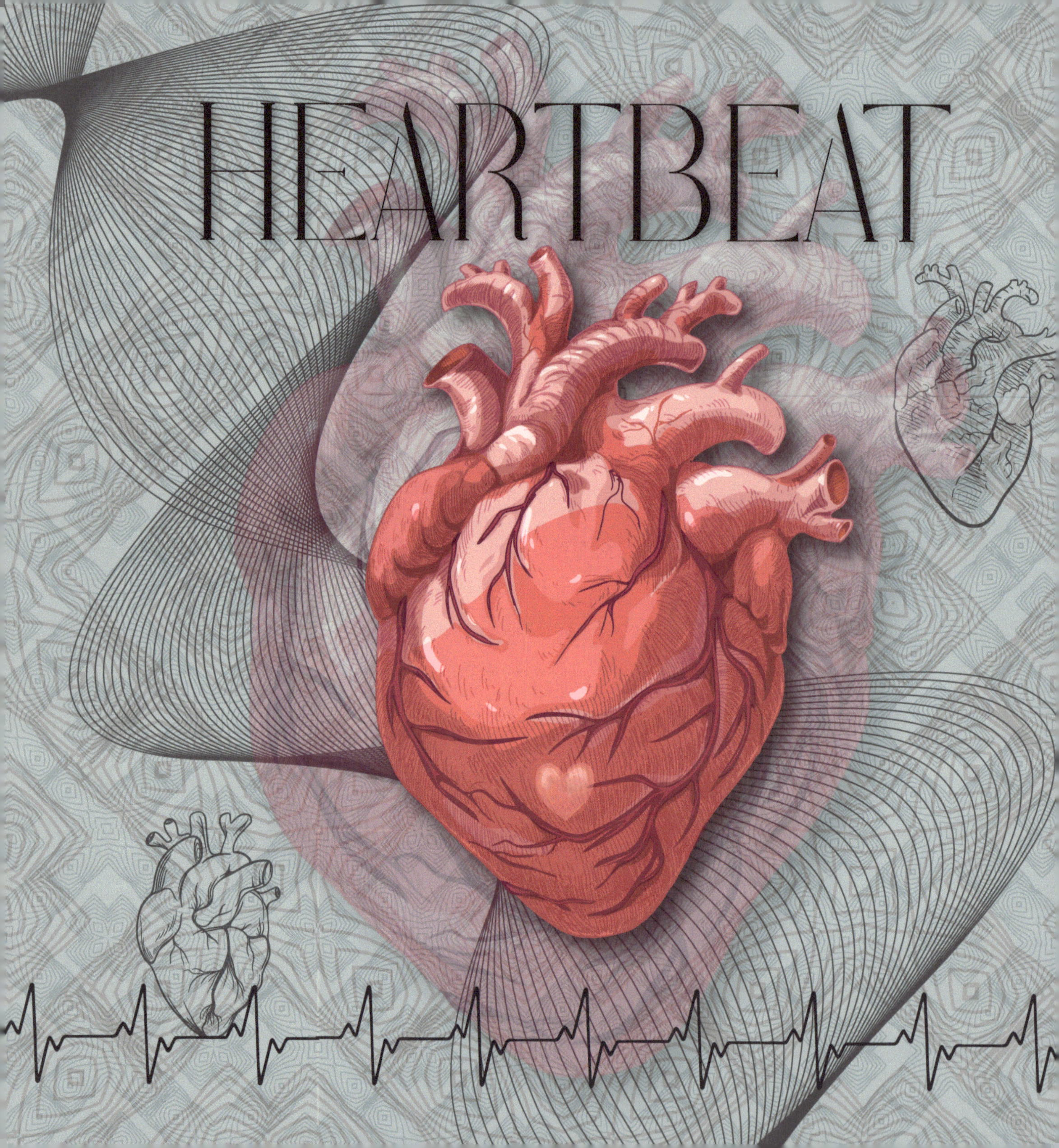
HEARTBEAT

Your heart's a drum that plays a song.
It keeps you going all day long.
It beats when you are fast or slow
and never stops its rhythmic flow.

When you wake or when you rest,
it taps a tune within your chest.
The Maker formed it deep inside—
a wondrous sign that you're alive!

BLUE EYES
BROWN HAIR
DNA
STRONG HEART
CREATIVITY
BOY OR GIRL
(determined at conception— this does not change)
BIG FEET

Each living thing, both big and small,
has DNA inside it all!
The Maker wrote it strand by strand—
breathed life into it, clearly planned.

It shapes the wing, the shell, the root,
the fur, the fin, the flower, the fruit!

Your DNA's a perfect plan—
a blueprint made when life began.
A swirling code that's all your own,
in every cell, it's clearly shown.

FINGERPRINT

PATTERNS

No one has patterns quite like you.
Unique are your fingerprints—yes, it's true.
The swirls and loops are one-of-a-kind—
a special stamp the Creator designed.

So check your hands, make sure they're true.
Leave prints of love in all you do!

HONEYCOMB

HEXAGON

Bees don't guess—they always know
how to make their pattern grow!
Each shape fits tight—no space to spare—
a perfect plan that's built with care!

The Maker gave them this smart way
to build their hives and work each day!

SPIRALS

Notice the curve in the petals and rows.
There's something grand that nature knows.
From snails that crawl to galaxies wide,
both tiny and huge, these spirals don't hide.

Each turn and curve is not by chance.
They swirl in life's creative dance!

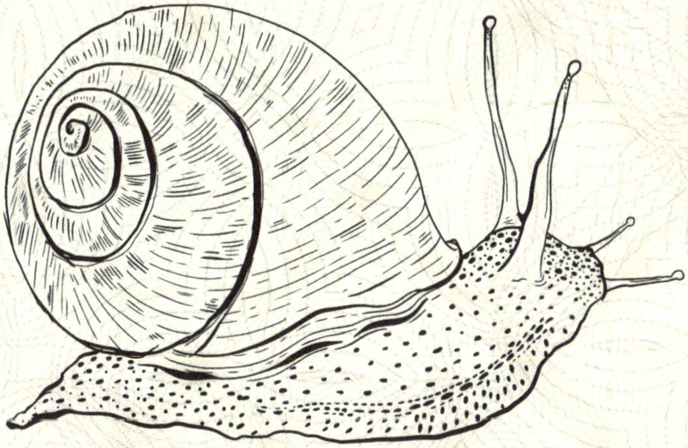

SHAPE & FORM

IN NATURE

Shapes are part of nature's song—
they've been in plain sight, all along!

A circular pattern in the ripple on a lake,
the segment of webbing a spider will make.
The shape of a heart in a redbud leaf,
the branching forms of the coral reef.

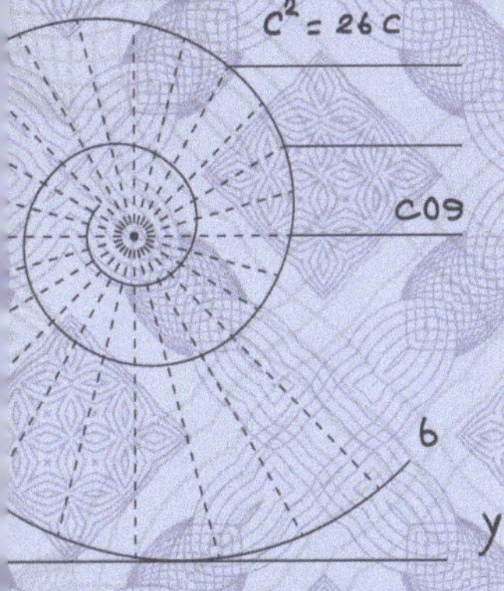

Each one speaks of perfect care—
the Maker placed them everywhere.

MATHEMATICS
IN NATURE

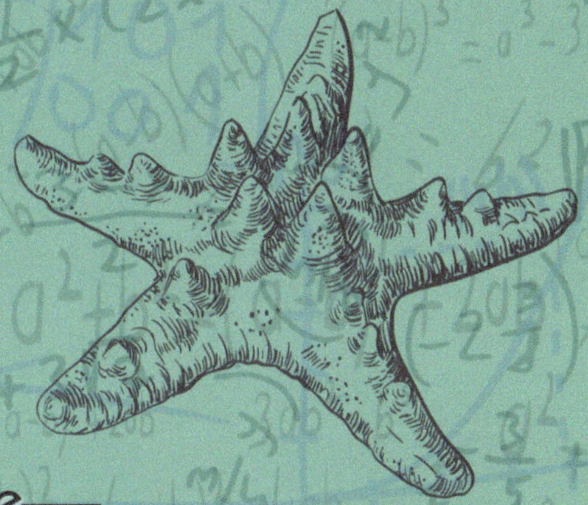

Circles, angles, lines so fine—
part of creation's grand design.
In buzzing bees and branching trees,
there's math at work in skies and seas.

The Maker formed it all with care—
a world of wonder everywhere!
So when you count or measure a space,
you're seeing glimpses of His grace!

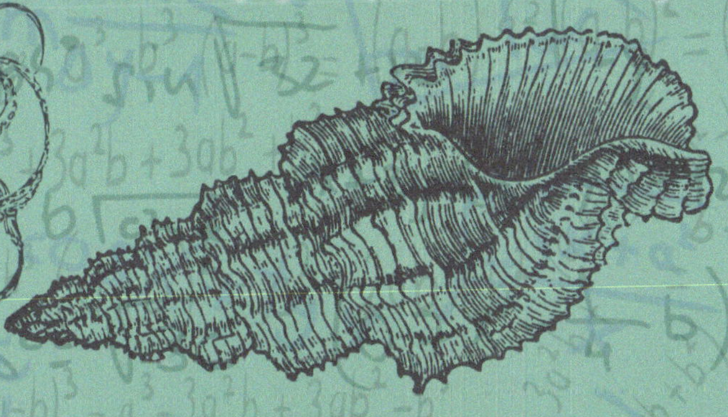
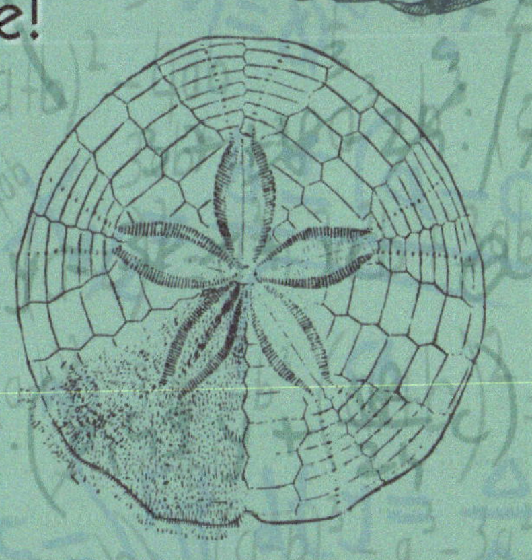

SYMMETRY

Butterfly wings are soft and light
with matching patterns, left and right.
They flutter gently through the breeze
and rest on flowers, grass, or trees.
The Maker made them bright and true—
each one a wonder, just like you!

SNOWFLAKE

RADIAL SYMMETRY

Snowflakes fall without a sound
spinning gently to the ground.
Each one special, shaped with care—
like fingerprints in frosty air!

The Creator makes them all brand-new
and sends them drifting down to you!

SEASONS

Spring makes blossoms, fresh and new—
summer skies are warm and blue.
Autumn leaves fall, crisp and bright—
winter sparkles, soft and white.
Each season comes with perfect care—
the Maker's touch is everywhere!

RHYTHM
OF REST

(6 ordinary days like black peppercorns and the 7th day special like a beautiful rose bud)

Our Maker worked for six full days
then showed us rest to bless our ways.
A weekly pause, a sacred space,
where peace and love and stillness grace.
The seventh day our Maker blessed—
the rhythm of our weekly rest!

APPOINTED

TIMES & REMEMBRANCES

WEEKLY SHABBAT
NEW MOON
PURIM
PASSOVER
UNLEAVENED BREAD
FIRSTFRUITS
COUNTING THE OMER
SHAVUOT
FEAST OF TRUMPETS
DAY OF ATONEMENT
SUKKOT
EIGHTH DAY
FEAST OF DEDICATION
SHEMITAH
YEAR OF JUBILEE

The King and Creator of everything
spoke and stirred the world to sing.
He made the stars, the moon, the sun,
to mark the times for everyone.

Each of His appointed times
all circle back through heavenly signs.
From springtime Feasts to those in fall,
His plan includes us, one and all!

Each cycle comes with joy and rest—
the Maker's rhythm is the best!

Our King and Creator, Your glory is grand.
Our lives are so blessed by Your loving hand.
Your purposes flow through all time and space,
revealing Your goodness, Your mercy, Your grace.
So thank You for shaping our lives with Your care,
for blessings abundant, for love everywhere.
May we walk in Your rhythm,
rejoice in Your ways,
and honor Your name
through all of our days.

"As long as the earth endures,
seedtime and harvest,
cold and heat,
summer and winter,
day and night
will never cease."
Genesis 8:22

"The day is Yours,
and Yours also the night;
You established the sun and moon.
It was You who set
all the boundaries of the earth;
You made both
summer and winter."
Psalm 74:16-17

... a note from the author ...

Every spiral, rhythm, and shape in nature reminds us of the Creator's perfect plan, His deep love for life, and His wisdom woven into all things.

Patterns are like the hidden language of creation. They weave through every corner of life, linking things that seem so different into one grand story. Whether we're looking at the swirl of a galaxy far away or the curl of a fern just outside our window, the same sense of order and purpose shines through. These designs are not random. They point to a Creator who built His love into every detail of His creation.

Take the Fibonacci sequence, for example—a simple string of numbers that shows up again and again in nature. Pinecones, sunflowers, seashells, hurricanes, and galaxies all carry its spiral fingerprint. It's as if the Creator has woven into the fabric of creation countless treasures, reminding us that He delights in both beauty and precision.

Even more astonishing, deep inside every living creature lies DNA—the most detailed pattern of all. This tiny code contains the instructions for life, written with more care than any library of books. Each strand whispers of a Designer who knows us intimately and who planned us before we took our first breath. Shapes, rhythms, and cycles fill creation like music fills a song. Together, they declare that life is not an accident. The same King and Creator who placed the stars in perfect order also lovingly shaped our fingerprints with unique design. Patterns remind us that He is both powerful and personal, sovereign and gracious—crafting the universe with mathematical brilliance and shaping our lives with tender love. Let's honor Him with our lives!

With awe and wonder,
Allison Eley

About Allison Eley

She's a wife and a mom and a Mimi too—
a writer of stories both joyful and true.
She loves to explore what the Creator has made—
in forests, in flowers, in sun and in shade.

Inspired by grandchildren who laugh, learn, and play,
she dreams up her books to brighten their way.
With beauty and faith in each line and each rhyme,
she points little hearts to a love that's divine.

Her hope is that children will look up and see
the Maker's design in a bird or a tree
and grow full of wonder with worship and grace
as they spot His fingerprints all over the place!

"You are worthy, our Lord and God, to receive glory and honor and power, for You created all things, and by Your will they were created and have their being."
Revelation 4:11

Books by Allison Eley

Little Learners—Big Creator

Animal ABCs

Counting Fun with Fruits & Veggies

Colors of Creation

Patterns on Purpose

Original Opposites

The Creator's Design

Yahweh's Rhythms & Reminders

Passover

Feast of Unleavened Bread

Feast of Firstfruits

Shavuot

Yom Teruah

Yom Kippur

Sukkot

The King's Calendar

Little Reminders

Shabbat Blessings

New Moon

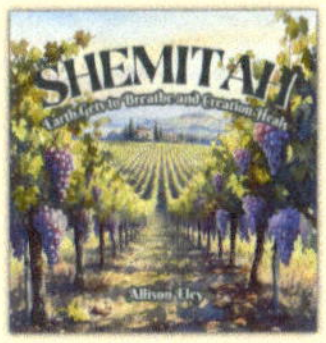

Shemitah

Hanukkah

Purim

P. Pie Penelope May

Mimi & P. Pie Penelope May

More to come in this series!

These and more beautiful books are carefully being shaped and formed! Discover the growing collection anytime!
eleypublishing.com

ELEY PUBLISHING

A Very Special Thank You

to every creator whose gifts radiate with light and life.
Thank you for weaving your unique design into this world.
Your work is a thread in the tapestry, a rhythm in the song, a pattern in the painting,
and a touch of beauty woven into the world, bringing blessing to others.

For permission requests, contact
Eley Publishing
eleypublishing@gmail.com
Ava, Missouri
Library of Congress Control Number: 2025911110
Paperback ISBN: 978-1-967834-06-8
Hardcover ISBN: 978-1-967834-07-5

ELEY
PUBLISHING

www.ingramcontent.com/pod-product-compliance
Ingram Content Group UK Ltd.
Pitfield, Milton Keynes, MK11 3LW, UK
UKHW061033310726
14089UKWH00010B/223
9781967834075